PORNification

by Andrew Benjamin

Published by Falls Media
565 Park Avenue, Suite 11E
New York, NY 10021

First Printing, May 2006
10 9 8 7 6 5 4 3 2
© Copyright Andrew Benjamin, 2006
All Rights Reserved

Printed in Canada
Design by Thomas Schirtz

ISBN 0-9740439-6-6

Table of Contents

Introduction

By the authors of *Would You Rather...?*®

Porn·i·fi·ca·tion:

noun, 1) the art of turning a legitimate film title into a porno by manipulating a word or group of words in the title, often employing the use of puns to create a lurid, sexually suggestive title; 2) a skill to make your parents proud

Pornography is everywhere (so I hear.) Hang around a newsstand for five minutes and you'll likely spy a patron blackening his fingers as he discretely tries to push the dark plastic covering to reveal the cover photo of Swank or any of the other 50 porn mags cluttering that top shelf.

Type in a few letters on a friend's browser, and watch the pornographic truth of his Internet history pop up.

But call us old-fashioned; we prefer the good old porno parody. The porn flick based on a major motion picture or the occasional TV show. It's a time-honored tradition dating back to *Bone With The Wind* and continuing to this day with films like *Butt-pirates of the Carribean*.

And while the films may be enjoyable themselves (so I hear), it's enough to browse a catalog, website, or video store shelf just to appreciate the titles. And it's even more fun to come up with one's own pornifications. With this in mind, we felt it our civic duty to help in the creation of this very important tome.

How To Use This Book

Many of the titles in this book are not actual produced porn movies. However, as the golden rule of pornification states...

FOR EVERY LEGIT MOVIE, THERE EXISTS (AT LEAST THEORETICALLY) A PORN VERSION OF THAT MOVIE.

On the left of the pages of this book, you'll find the original movie titles; on the right, you will see its corresponding pornification. Read for your own amusement and/or quiz your friends by reciting the original title and see if they can come up with the pornifications.

There are many other quizzes, features, and challenges in this book to test your word agility and level of debauchery. So go ahead and share a guilty laugh as you simultaneously rest and engage your mind and enter the world of PORNIFICATION!

5 Great Games To Play With Pornification

In addition to the quizzes, there are number of ways to play games with this book.

Shout-Out: The pornifications we've offered are not the only right answers. There are no wrong answers in *Pornification*; actually, they are all "wrong" in a sense. But there are no incorrect answers. So, a fun game to play is for one reader to say the original movie title and to have players yell out pornifications until the answers in the book are named. First player to name a title listed in the book wins. Let the titles fly fast and furious.

Pornification Charades: Play charades with the pornified title. First, somebody acts out the words to the pornified title. After the pornified title has been called out word-for-word, guessers then have to determine the original title. The first player or team to shout out the original title wins. Hilarity will ensue.[1]

Best Title/Most Titles: Mention a movie title. Steal a timer from Boggle or some other game and have everyone write down possible pornifications. After time is up, share your titles. Award a winner for most titles and best title.

---

[1]Hilarity not guaranteed

IMAGINE THE PLOT: Though plot is becoming an obsolete word in both mainstream and adult film, the great porn movies still have a storyline, a wonderfully inane storyline. Play the part of porn screenwriter and suggest a plotline. If the pornification is "Diddler on the Roof" for example, you might suggest the plot concerns a "peeping tom who pleasures himself on the rooftops of a Jewish village."

FOR THE AUTOPORN SECTIONS: see how many already-dirty-sounding titles you can name.

PLAY WITH YOURSELF

There are plenty of quizzes to play by yourself, and the book can of course be read purely for humor, so if this book is your only friend, it's okay.

chapter 1

PORNIFICATION 101

ORIGINAL TITLE	PORNification
The Nutty Professor ⟶	*The Slutty Professor*
Cold Mountain ⟶	*Cold Mountin'*
Curious George ⟶	*Bi-Curious George, Curious Gorge*

ORIGINAL TITLE	PORNification
Aint Misbehavin' ⟶	*Taint Misbehavin'*
Glory ⟶	*Glory Hole*
Finding Nemo ⟶	*Grinding Nemo*

ORIGINAL TITLE	PORNification
Toy Story ⟶	*Boy Story*
	Sex Toy Story (CGI)
The Right Stuff ⟶	*The White Stuff,*
	The Right Stiff,
	The Tight Muff
S.W.A.T ⟶	*T.W.A.T*

T&A: De-pornification

(Tests & Answers)

Here are some pornified titles. Can you figure out the original Hollywood film that inspired them?

American Booty

Titty Lickers

Jugsy

Swallow Hal

White Men Can't Hump

Answers:

American Beauty - City Slickers - Bugsy - Shallow Hal - White Men Can't Jump

13

ORIGINAL TITLE	PORNification
Big Trouble in Little China ⟶	*Big Trouble in Little Vagina*
King Kong ⟶	*King Dong*
Space Jam ⟶	*Face Jam*

T^{ests}&A^{nswers:} The Porns of Star Wars

Long, long ago, in a galaxy far away, sci-fi nerds substituted porn for actually dating women. Can you pornify the Star Wars series?

Answers on the following page.

Episode IV - A New Hope

Episode V - The Empire Strikes Back

Episode VI - Return of the Jedi

Episode I - The Phantom Menace

Episode II - Attack of the Clones

Episode III - Revenge of the Sith

T&A ests nswers: Star Whores!

Episode IV – A New Hole

Episode V – The Empire Strokes Back

Episode VI – Return of the Red-eye

Episode I – The Phantom Penis, The Phantom Anus

Episode II – Attack of the Bones

Episode III – Revenge of the Tith (lisp fetish)

Featuring BenWa Kenobi, Hand Solo, the Perineum Falcon, the robot DP-AP, and the wise and wrinkly Scrota.

ORIGINAL TITLE	PORNification
Pearl Harbor →	*Pearl Necklace Harbor*
Master and Commander →	*Blast Her and Command Her*
You've Got Mail →	*You've Got She-male*

PORNIFICATION 101

Auto-Porn

(because some films come pre-pornified)

Shaft

Snatch

Big Daddy

Eight is Enough

Three's Company

Driving Miss Daisy

Big

Blown Away

Free Willy

ORIGINAL TITLE	PORNification
Dirty Harry ⟶	*Dirty, Hairy*
Gladiator ⟶	*Glad-he-ate-her*
Ocean's 11 ⟶	*Ocean's 11 Inches*

∫hake∫Porn!

A Midsummer Night's Cream

All's Well That Rear Ends Well

Much Ado About Nutting

As She Likes It

Julius Creamer, Julius Seize Her

King Rear

Macbreast

Pleasure for Pleasure

Coriol's Anus

Ramlet

Bordello

Homeo & Julio

The Merchants of Penis

The Taming of the Screw

The Temptress

Twelve Inch Knight

Two Gentlemen in Veronica

A Midsummer Night's Wet Dream

T_{ests}&A_{nswers}: The Porns of Stephen Spielberg

Can you pornify the fantasies made from the master of fantasy, himself, Stephen Spielberg?

Saving Private Ryan

Jurassic Park

Schindler's List

E.T. The Extra Terrestrial

Answers:

Saving Ryan's Privates/Shaving Private Ryan - Jurassic Pork - Schindler's Fist - E.T. The Extra Testicle

ORIGINAL TITLE	PORNification
The Little Mermaid →	*The Little Sperm Maid*
Pay it Forward →	*Spray it Forward*
Everybody Loves Raymond →	*Everybody Loves Rimmin'*

Fetish 101

ORIGINAL TITLE

PORNification

The Bridget Jones Diaries → The Midget Bones Diaries (little people)

Dungeons and Dragons → Dungeons & Drag Queens (domination)

Three Men and a Baby → Three Men and A Maybe (she-male)

Married to the Mob → Married to the Knob (oral)

chapter **2**

ACTION

ORIGINAL TITLE	PORNification
Gone in Sixty Seconds ⟶	*Done in Sixty Seconds,* *Done in Sloppy Seconds*
Mission Impossible ⟶	*Emission Possible,* *Submission Impossible,* *Missionary Impossible*
Collateral Damage ⟶	*Clitoral Rammage*

ORIGINAL TITLE	PORNification
The Fast and the Furious ⟶	*The Fast and Bicurious*
Tomb Raider ⟶	*Womb Raider*
Lethal Weapon ⟶	*Lethal Strap-on, Urethral Weapon*

ACTION

ORIGINAL TITLE	PORNification
Pirates of the Carribean: The Curse of the Black Pearl →	*Butt Pirates of the Caribbean: The Curse of the Black Pearl Necklace*
The Fugitive →	*The Spooge-ative*
Charlie's Angels: Full Throttle →	*Charlie's Anals: Full Butthole*

James Bondage Films

Dr. Yes

Poonraker

For Your Thighs Only

Brownfinger

Thunderballs

You Only Give Twice

Live and Let Dyke

License to Drill

GoldenShowerEye

Hymens Are Forever

Cock-to-pussy

Teens Who Never Say Never Again

ACTION

29

ORIGINAL TITLE	PORNification
I-spy ⟶	*Brown-eye Spy, Pie Spy*
The French Connection ⟶	*The French Erection, The French Tickler Connection*
Face/Off ⟶	*Face/On, Facial/Off, Jerk/Off*

Hung Fu

ORIGINAL TITLE	PORNification
Enter the Dragon ⟶	*Enter the Drag Queen*
Legend of the Drunken Master ⟶	*Legend of Spunkin' Master, Legend of the Drunken Masturbator*
Kill Bill ⟶	*Fill Bill, Drill Jill*

T^{ests}&A^{nswers}: Comic Book Heroes

Here are the plots of three pornified comic-book hero movies. Can you give the title to the plot described and the original movie it is based on?
Answers on the following page.

Two tight-wearing heroes work closely together exploring one's cave; repressed homo-erotic urges are finally realized with the help of utility belts of sex toys.

"You wouldn't like me when I'm horny" says Bruce Boner, as his state of sexual arousal causes his penis to become green and massively engorged.

These mutants have unusual powers such as a perpetual erection, the ability to ejaculate enormous distances, and a retractable penis and long endurance. Characters include: Wolveream, Sperm, Cyclops (autoporn), and Professor XXX.

Answers:

Batman and Robin ⟶ Buttman and Throbbin'

The Incredible Hulk ⟶ The Incredible Bulk,
The Incredible Bulge,
The Incredible Yolk

X-Men ⟶ XXX-Men, Sexmen

ACTION

ORIGINAL TITLE	PORNification
Mad Max: Road Warrior →	Mad Maxxx: Load Warrior
The Italian Job →	The Italian Handjob, The Italian Blowjob, The Genitalian Job
The Mummy →	The Cummy, The Milf

ORIGINAL TITLE	PORNification
The Fantastic Four ⟶	*The Fantastic Whore,* *The Fantastic Foursome*
Superman ⟶	*Schtuperman,* *Superglans*
V for Vendetta ⟶	*V for Vagina*

ACTION

Auto-Porn

(because some films come pre-pornified)

Dick Tracy

Deep Impact

The Firm

XXX

The Dirty Dozen

Bad Boys

ORIGINAL TITLE	PORNification
Witness →	*Wetness, Splitness*
Pulp Fiction →	*Pulp Friction, Gulp Friction, Pump Friction*
The Perfect Storm →	*The Perfect Sperm*

ACTION

ORIGINAL TITLE	PORNification
Little Big Man →	*Big Little Man* (midget fetish)
Presumed Innocent →	*Pre-cum'ed Innocent,* *Consumed Innocent*
Stake Out →	*Stinkout, Stake In,* *Steak In*

T^{ests}&A^{nswers}: Match the Actor

Match the "pornified" action star to their not so well known movies:
Answers on the following page.

Clint Eatwood	*The Bum of All Rears, Baredevil*
Bruce Willie	*The Porn Supremacy, Pounders*
Ben Asslick	*Constant Teen, The 'Natrix*
Ke-on-yo Knees	*Every Which Way in the Can*
Matt Semen	*Guy Hard With a Vengeance*

T^{ests} & A^{nswers}: Match the Actor

Answers:

Clint Eatwood (Eastwood) – Every Which Way In The Can
(Every Which Way You Can)

Bruce Willie (Willis) – Guy Hard with a Vengeance
(Die Hard with a Vengeance)

Ben Asslick (Affleck) – The Bum of All Rears (The Sum
of All Fears), Baredevil (Daredevil)

Ke-on-yo Knees (Keanu Reeves) – Constant Teen (Constantine),
The 'Natrix (The Matrix)

Matt Semen (Damon) – The Porn Supremacy (The Bourne
Supremacy), Pounders (Rounders)

ORIGINAL TITLE	PORNification
Training Day ⟶	*Draining Day,* *Straining Day,* *Staining Day*
Bullitt ⟶	*Pullitt*
Natural Born Killers ⟶	*Natural Porn Spillers*

ACTION

ORIGINAL TITLE	PORNification
Collateral ⟶	*Ho Lateral*
The Great Escape ⟶	*The Great Assgape* (sorry, Mom)
Himalaya ⟶	*Him'll Lay Ya*

100% REAL (Actual Produced Porns)

A Civil Action	*A Penile Action*
Goldeneye	*Brown Eye*
Clear and Present Danger	*A Rear and Pleasant Dangler, Clear and Present Dangler*
Goonies	*Poonies*
Batman	*Splatman*
The Hunt for Red October	*The Hunt for Miss October, The Hunt for Pink October*
Romancing the Stone	*Romancing the Bone*
Reservoir Dogs	*Reservoir Bitches*

ACTION

ORIGINAL TITLE	PORNification
The Last Boy Scout ⟶	*The Last Boy Spout*
Hollywood Homicide ⟶	*Hollywood Spermicide*
The Last Samurai ⟶	*The Ass Slamurai*

ORIGINAL TITLE	PORNification
Indiana Jones and the Temple of Doom ⟶	*In Diana Jones and the Temple of Poon*
National Treasure ⟶	*Nat's Anal Treasure*
Conan the Barbarian ⟶	*Bonin' the Librarian*

ACTION

45

T&A

T_{ests} & A_{nswers}: Something in Common

What do these pornified titles have in common?

Answers found below.

First Pud

Tango and Gash

Stop or My Mom Will Squirt

Rambone

Cocky

Clitbanger

Answers:

They are all Sylvester Stabone movies. *First Blood* - *Tango and Cash* - *Stop Or My Mom Will Shoot* - *Rambo* - *Rocky* - *Cliffhanger*

46

All-Natural Disasters

ORIGINAL TITLE	PORNification
Twister ⟶	*Twist Her, Fister*
Volcano ⟶	*Vulvano*
Armageddon ⟶	*Armageddingiton*

ACTION

47

All is Fair in Lust and War

Money quotes from military movies.

Top Cum (*Top Gun*)

"I feel the need, the need for a quickie."

A Cock and Lips Now (*Apocalypse Now*)

"I love the smell of KY in the morning."

A Few Goo'd Men (*A Few Good Men*)

"You want the spooge? You can't handle the spooge!"

Fetish: ʃhe-maleʃ

(To Each His and/or Her Own.)

ORIGINAL TITLE	PORNification
Mighty Aphrodite	*Mighty Hermaphrodite*
Two and a Half Men	autoporn
The Transporter	*The Transporker*
Eat, Drink, Man, Woman	*Eat/drink Man/woman*
Strangers On A Train	*Strangers On A Tranny*

chapter **3**

ANIMATION

ORIGINAL TITLE	PORNification
101 Dalmatians! ⟶	*101 All-Asians!* *101 Lacatations!*
Robin Hood ⟶	*Throbbin' Wood*
Alladin ⟶	*A Lad In*

ORIGINAL TITLE	PORNification
The Fox and the Hound →	*The Foxxe and Her Mound*
Pocahontas →	*Poke-a-hot-ass*
Dumbo →	*Dumbone, Jumbo*

ANIMATION

ORIGINAL TITLE		PORNification
Sleeping Beauty	→	*Seeping Booty*
Rudyard Kipling's The Jungle Book	→	*Pudyard Kipling's The Bung-hole Book*
The Incredibles	→	*The Pink Edibles, The Incrediballs*

The Orgasmic World of Dr. Leuss

The Splat in the Hat

The Wench Who Screwed XXXMAS

Hop on Pop (autoporn)

One Tit, Two Tit, Red Tit, Blue Tit

The Whorax

Horton Bangs a Who

Oh! The Places You'll Blow

There's a Rocket in my Pocket

Yertle The Squirtle

ORIGINAL TITLE	PORNification
The Hunchback of Notre Dame →	*The Hung-black of Notre Dame*
Fantasia →	*Fantasians, Fantasia Carrera*
Casper →	*Gasper*

ORIGINAL TITLE	PORNification
A Bug's Life ⟶	*A Buggerer's Life,* *A Tug's Life,* *A Plug's Life*
Monsters, Inc. ⟶	*Monsters' Ink,* *Monster Stink,* *Monster Pink*
Rugrats ⟶	*Rugrash*

ORIGINAL TITLE	PORNification
Who Framed Roger Rabbit ⟶	*Who Rimmed Roger Rabbit?*
Inspector Gadget ⟶	*Inspect Her Gadget*
Bambi ⟶	*Wham-Bambi*

ORIGINAL TITLE	PORNification
Shrek →	*Schtup, Shmeg*
The Lion King →	*The Loin King*
You're a Good Man Charlie Brown →	*You're a Good Fuck Charlie Brown*

ANIMATION

Tests & Answers: Soundtracks

Can you name the movie in whose soundtrack these songs appear?

Answers on the following page.

See Our Breasts

The Circle Jerk of Life

Someday My Prince Will Come (autoporn)

When You Wish Upon a Chocolate Starfish

Answers:

Be Our Guest – Booty and the Beast (Beauty and the Beast)

The Circle of Life – The Loin King (The Lion King)

Some Day My Prince Will Come – Snow White and the Seven Whores (Dwarves)

When You Wish Upon a Star – Bukkakeo (Pinnochio)

ORIGINAL TITLE	PORNification
Cinderella ⟶	*Fingersmella*
Howl's Moving Castle ⟶	*Howl's Moving Asshole*
Chicken Run ⟶	*Chicken Choke*

Fetiʃh: ʃcat

(scatalogical)

ORIGINAL TITLE	PORNification
Hoop Dreams	Poop Dreams
Four Weddings and A Funeral	Four Wettings and a Funnel
The Princess Diaries	The Princess Diarrheas
Speed	Peed
Enemy of the State	Enema of the State
Quantum Leap	Quantum Leak
On Golden Pond	In Golden Pond
Trading Places	Trading Feces
The Green Mile	The Green Pile

chapter **4**

CLASSICS

ORIGINAL TITLE	PORNification
Thanks For the Memories →	*Thanks For the Mammaries*
The Last Emperor →	*The Last Enterer*
The Deer Hunter →	*The Rear Hunter, The Rear Humper*

ORIGINAL TITLE	PORNification
Out of Africa ⟶	*In and Out of Africa*
My Left Foot ⟶	*My Left Nut,* *My Left Foot Fetish*
The Silence of *the Lambs* ⟶	*The Science of* *the Lamb Skin,* *The Silence of* *the Clams*

CLASSICS

ORIGINAL TITLE	PORNification
Terms of Endearment ⟶	*Sperms of Endearment,* *Terms of Endowment*
Kramer vs. Kramer ⟶	*Cummer vs. Cummer,* *Creamer vs. Creamer*
Titanic ⟶	*Tit-antics,* *Tightanus*

ORIGINAL TITLE	**PORNification**
All About Eve ⟶	*All Over Eve*
Around the World in Eighty Days ⟶	*Around the World in Eighty Lays*
The English Patient ⟶	*The Cunnilingus Patient*

CLASSICS

ORIGINAL TITLE	PORNification
The Godfather ⟶	*The Goofather,* *The Rodfather,* *The Wadfather*
One Flew Over the *Cuckoo's Nest* ⟶	*One Spewed Over the* *Cuckoo's Breast*
Mutiny on the Bounty ⟶	*Mutiny on the Booty*

Tests & Answers: Movie Plots

Name the pornification for the theoretical plots below.
Answers found below.

A paranoid schizophrenic math genius hallucinates having sex with imaginary partners.

A man paints his penis blue and orange and leads his band of men into an orgy.

A paranoid schizophrenic math genius hallucinates having anal sex with imaginary partners.

Answers:

A Beautiful Grind - Brave-Hard-on - A Beautiful Behind

ORIGINAL TITLE	PORNification
The Sting ⟶	*The Stink,* *The Fling*
The Grapes of Wrath ⟶	*The Gapes of Wrath*
The Wizard of Oz ⟶	*The Jizzer of Ooze,* *The Wizard of Aaaahs*

ORIGINAL TITLE		PORNification
Ben-Hur	$\longrightarrow$	*Bend-Her*
Citizen Kane	$\longrightarrow$	*Sit on His Cane*
Dr. Strangelove	$\longrightarrow$	*Dr. Strangeglove, Dr. Strangelust*

CLASSICS

ORIGINAL TITLE	PORNification
Lawrence of Arabia ⟶	*Florence of A Labia,* *Torrents from her Labia*
Chariots of Fire ⟶	*Cherries on Fire,* *Cheri Tits on Fire*
Arabian Nights ⟶	*Arabian Goggles Night* (google it)

T^{ests} & A^{nswers}: The Master of Suspense

With movies like *The Pleasure Garden* and *The Young and the Innocent*, the pre-pornified Alfred Hitchcock seemed to get off on suggestive titles. Can you finish the job and pornify the following titles from the Master of Suspense? Answers on the following page.

The Man Who Knew Too Much
Psycho
Dial M for Murder
Rear Window
North By Northwest
To Catch a Thief
The Wrong Man
Strangers on a Train
The Birds

T_{ests}&A_{nswers}: The Master of Suspense

Answers:

The Man Who Screwed Too Much
Dyke Ho
Dial S&M To Hurt Her
Rear Window (autoporn)
Peter North By Randy West
To Snatch a Queef
The Long Man
Strangers in a Train
The Beads

ORIGINAL TITLE	PORNification
The Maltese Falcon ⟶	*The Ball-Tease Falcon, The Maltese Phallus*
The Treasure of the Sierra Madre ⟶	*The Pleasure of the Su Hairy Madre*
Patton ⟶	*Splattin'*

ORIGINAL TITLE	PORNification
Camelot ⟶	*Cameltoe*
Chinatown ⟶	*'Ginatown*
The Glass Menagerie ⟶	*The Glass Menage a Trois, The Ass Menagerie*

ORIGINAL TITLE		PORNification
Rashomon	⟶	*Rasho-mons Pubis*
Das Boot	⟶	*Das Boob,* *Das Booty*
The Great Dictator	⟶	*The Great Dick Taster*

CLASSICS

ORIGINAL TITLE	PORNification
Guess Who's Coming To Dinner ⟶	*Guess Who's Cumming at Dinner*
Fargo ⟶	*Gofar*
Children of a Lesser God ⟶	*Children of a Leather God*

Question to ponder: How would dirty talk function in a deaf porno?

Fetish: Feet

ORIGINAL TITLE   PORNification

Tootsie   *Footsie*

Shawshank Redemption   *Shoeshank Redemption*

In Her Shoes   (autoporn)

Wheel of Fortune   *Heels of Fortune*

Raiders of the Lost Ark   *Raiders of the Lost Arch*

chapter **5**

COMEDY

ORIGINAL TITLE	PORNification
Must Love Dogs →	*Must Love Doggie Style*
Legally Blonde →	*Barely Legally Blonde, Legally Bound*
O' Brother, Where Art Thou? →	*O' Brothel, Where Art Thou?*

ORIGINAL TITLE	PORNification
Smokey and the Bandit →	*Smoke Me and Demand It*
The Graduate →	*The Grad You Ate*
Daddy Day Care →	*Who's Your Daddy Day Care, Pimp Daddy Day Care*

COMEDY

ORIGINAL TITLE	PORNification
Good Morning, Vietnam	*Good Moaning, Vietnam, Good Morning, Vietnamese Girl*
How to Lose a Guy in Ten Days	*How to Please a Guy in Ten Ways*
Being John Malkovich	*Being John Holmes*

T^{ests} & A^{nswers}: Got Woody?

With a name like "Woody", Mr. Allen is begging to have his films pornified. Try your hand at turning "a neurotic film" into "an erotic film." Answers found below.

Hannah and Her Sisters

Sweet and Low Down

Hollywood Ending

Sleeper

Manhattan

Answers:

Hannah Does Her Sisters, Sweet and Down Low, Hollywood Happy Ending, Seeper, Man-eatin'

COMEDY

ORIGINAL TITLE	PORNification
Mary Poppins ⟶	*Cherry Poppin's*
Nanny McPhee ⟶	*Punanny McPhee*
The Pacifier ⟶	*The Gratifier, The Assifier*

ORIGINAL TITLE	PORNification
Sliding Doors ⟶	*Sliding Backdoors*
Broadcast News ⟶	*Broadcast Spews*
Elf ⟶	*Milf,* *Self*

COMEDY

ORIGINAL TITLE		PORNification
Anchorman	⟶	*Wankerman*
Cheaper by the Dozen	⟶	*Deeper by the Dozen*
Roger & Me	⟶	*Rogerin' Me*

T_{ests} & A_{nswers}: "All-Tighty Then!"

Can you pornify these Jim Carrey movies to make them into gay porn films? Answers found below.

Ace Ventura Pet Detective

The Truman Show

Fun with Dick and Jane

The Cable Guy

COMEDY

Answers:

Ass Venturer: Butt Detective - The True Man Show - Fun With Dick and Vein - The Guy's Cable

91

ORIGINAL TITLE	PORNification
Fletch ⟶	*Felch*
Analyze This ⟶	*Analize This*
The Addams Family ⟶	*The Addams Family Jewels, The Madam's Family*

ORIGINAL TITLE	PORNification
There's Something About Mary →	*There's Something* (insert preposition) *Mary*
This is Spinal Tap →	*This is Anal Tap*
Dazed and Confused →	*Glazed and Abused*

COMEDY

John Huge Films

Sixteen Fondles

Spray Anything

The Fake Breast Club

Stains, Veins, and Autofellatios

Pretty in Pink (autoporn)

ORIGINAL TITLE		PORNification
Dr. Dolittle	⟶	*Dr. Do-a-lot*
George of the Jungle	⟶	*George of the Hung Well, Gorge of the Bunghole*
I ♥ Huckabees	⟶	*I ➤ Huckabees*

ORIGINAL TITLE	PORNification
Liar Liar ⟶	*Lay Her, Lay Her*
9 to 5 ⟶	*Nine Inches to Five Women*
Network ⟶	*Nutwork*

ORIGINAL TITLE	PORNification
When Harry Met Sally →	*When Harry Ate Sally*
The Big Chill →	*The Big Dill*
Love Actually →	*Lust, Actually, Upon Further Consideration*

COMEDY

The Pornifications of Steve Martin

Swapgirl

The Jerk-off

The Pink Poonther

Glowfinger

The Man With Two Hanging Brains

All Over Me

Coxxxanne, Roxoffe

ORIGINAL TITLE	PORNification
Adam's Rib ⟶	*Adam's Rub*
Monty Python and the Holy Grail ⟶	*Monty's Python in her Holy Grail*
Lost in Translation ⟶	*Lost in Transvestite, Lost in Ejaculation, Tossed in Penn Station*

COMEDY

ORIGINAL TITLE	PORNification
Soapdish ⟶	*Soaped Gish*
Zoolander ⟶	*Spew Lander*
Young Frankenstein ⟶	*Hung Frankenstein*

ORIGINAL TITLE	PORNification
How Stella Got Her Groove Back ⟶	*How Stella Got Her Tube Packed*
My Big Fat Greek Wedding ⟶	*My Big Fat Greek* (insert noun of your choice)
Three Men and A Baby ⟶	*Three Men and a Booby*

COMEDY

T^{ests}&A_{nswers}: Fun with Words

What word turns all of these into pornifications? Answers found below.

Big _____.

A _____ *Called Wanda*

Gone _____ *ing*

Prelude to a _____

Hannah and Her _____ *ers.*

One last hint, it was in the first chapter:
Schindler's _____

Answer:

First

ORIGINAL TITLE		PORNification
Two Weeks Notice	→	*Two Cheeks Crevice*
The World According to Garp	→	*The World According to Slurp*
The Longest Yard	→	*The Longest Hard-On*

COMEDY

ORIGINAL TITLE	PORNification
Office Space →	*Orifice Space*
Blazing Saddles →	*Blazing Straddles*
Dirty Rotten Scoundrels →	*Dirty Rotten Sanchez*

ORIGINAL TITLE	**PORNification**
Throw Momma From the Train →	*Throw Momma In A Train* (MILF fetish)
Tommy-Knockers →	*Mommy-Knockers* (MILF fetish)
Parenthood →	*Parentwood* (rare FILF fetish)

T^{ests} & A^{nswers}: Who You Gonna' Ball?

Which of the following pornifications of Ghost Busters were actually produced?

Answers found below.

Ghost Lusters	*Spermbusters*
Gangbusters	*Bra Busters*
Girl Busters	*Assbusters*
Nut Busters	*Ball Busters*
Butt Busters	

Answer:

All are real.

Fetish: Ethnic

ORIGINAL TITLE

PORNification

Seven Years in Tibet → Seven Years in Thai Butt

Jumpin' Jack Flash → Humpin' Black Flesh

Entourage → Into Raj

Hard Boiled → Hard Moyeled

The Lion, The Witch, and → The Mayan, the Bitch, and
the Wardrobe → the Cornhole

chapter **6**

DRAMA

ORIGINAL TITLE	PORNification
What Dreams May Come →	*Wet Dreams May Come*
Driving Miss Daisy →	*Riding Miss Daisy, Driving Miss Daisy Chain, Piledriving Miss Daisy*
12 Angry Men →	*12" Angry Men, 12 Horny Men*

ORIGINAL TITLE	PORNification
Dreamcatcher ⟶	*Creamcatcher*
The Bone Collector ⟶	*The Bone Erector*
Fatal Attraction ⟶	*Facial Attraction*

ORIGINAL TITLE	PORNification
Malcolm X ⟶	Malcolm XXX
Good Will Hunting ⟶	Good Will Humping, Good Milf Hunting
Regarding Henry ⟶	Regarding Hiney

T_{ests} & A_{nswers}: De-pornification

De-pornify the following dramas.
Answers found below.

An Orifice and a Genitalman

Hardened State

Throb Toy

Secretions and Sighs

DRAMA

Answers:

ORIGINAL TITLE	PORNification
Vanilla Sky ⟶	*Vanilla Eye*
Monster's Ball ⟶	*Monster Balls*
Se7en ⟶	*SeXen,* *Ei8ht*

ORIGINAL TITLE	PORNification
Six Degrees of Separation ⟶	*Six Degrees Of Penetration*
Waiting to Exhale ⟶	*Waiting to Impale, Waiting to Inhale*
Fear and Loathing in Las Vegas ⟶	*Queer and Blowing in Las Vegas*

DRAMA

T^{ests} & A^{nswers}: Feel Good Films

Can you pornify these "feel-good" movies into "feel-great" movies? Answers found below.

Mr. Holland's Opus

Remember the Titans

Patch Adams

Mona Lisa Smile

Answers:

Mr. Holland's Anus, Remember the Tight Ones, Snatch Adams, Mona Lisa Vertical Smile

ORIGINAL TITLE	PORNification
Punch Drunk Love ⟶	*Donkey-punch Drunk Love, Cum Drunk Love*
Beloved ⟶	*Bi-loved, Begloved*
The Professional ⟶	*The Amateur*

DRAMA

Knobster Flicks

ORIGINAL TITLE	PORNification
Gangs of New York →	*Gangbangs of New York*
Goodfellas →	*Goodfellatio*
Scarface →	*Scatface*

Auto-Porn
(because some films come "pre-pornified")

Stand and Deliver

Grand Canyon

Blow

Marathon Man

Boyz n the Hood

ORIGINAL TITLE	PORNification
Munich ⟶	*Eunuch*
Bonfire of the Vanities ⟶	*Bonfire in the Panties*
Dangerous Liaisons ⟶	*Dangerously Asians*

The Films of Crammin' Crow

Almost Anus

Vanilla Cream-Pie

Swingles

Spray Anything

ORIGINAL TITLE	PORNification
You Got Served →	*You Got Perved*
Pushing Tin →	*Pushing It In*
21 Grams →	*21 Slams,* *21 Cubic Centimeters*

ORIGINAL TITLE	PORNification
JFK ⟶	*J F's K*
Dead Man Walking ⟶	*Dead Man Wanking*
Meet Joe Black ⟶	*Joe Black Meat*

DRAMA

ORIGINAL TITLE	PORNification
The Legend of Bagger Vance	The Legend of Teabagger Vance, The Legend In Bagger's Pants
The Constant Gardener	The Instant Hardener
The Secret of My Success	The Secret of My Suck Sex

T_{ests}&A_{nswers}: Fun with Words

Fill in the blank to turn these titles into pornifications?
Answers found below.

A Time to _____

_____ *Bill: with Volume 2*

_____ *More Girls*

Answer:

It was there all along: "Fill" in the blank.

ORIGINAL TITLE	PORNification
Scent of A Woman ⟶	*Descent of a Woman*
Million Dollar Baby ⟶	*Million Dollar Labia*
Bright Lights, Big City ⟶	*Bright Lights, Big Titties*

ORIGINAL TITLE	PORNification
The Untouchables ⟶	*The Touchables*
You Can Count on Me ⟶	*You Can* (insert verb) *on Me*
Fight Club ⟶	*Cat Fight Club*

DRAMA

ORIGINAL TITLE	PORNification
Cool Hand Luke ⟶	*Warm Hand Luke,* *Cool Handjob Luke*
All the President's Men ⟶	*All the President's Semen*
Clockers ⟶	*Shockers*

ORIGINAL TITLE	PORNification
Cape Fear ⟶	*Cape Rear,* *Cape Queer,* *Gape Fear*
Requiem for a Dream ⟶	*Rectum for a Ream*
Maria Full of Grace ⟶	*Maria Full of Face,* *Maria Full of Disgrace*

DRAMA

Name the movies described below.

The Plot (such as it is): A retired cumslinger realizes that there is nothing left that he won't do. Co-stars Gene Rackman & Organ Freeman.

The Plot (such as it is): An up-and-coming young porn star finds a mentor to help break into the business, becomes disillusioned, and ultimately betrays him. The Money Quote: "Peed is good."

Answers:

Unforbidden, Ball Street

ORIGINAL TITLE	PORNification
A Very Large Engagement →	*A Very Large Engorgement*
Bugsy →	*Jugsy*
Eyes Wide Shut →	*Eyes Glued Shut*

DRAMA

Fetish: Menstruation

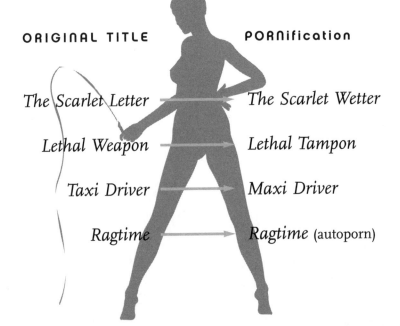

ORIGINAL TITLE

PORNification

The Scarlet Letter → *The Scarlet Wetter*

Lethal Weapon → *Lethal Tampon*

Taxi Driver → *Maxi Driver*

Ragtime → *Ragtime* (autoporn)

chapter **7**

SCI-FI/HORROR

ORIGINAL TITLE		PORNification
Interview With a Vampire	→	*Intercourse with a Vampire*
A.I.	→	*B.I.*
Minority Report	→	*Sorority Report*

ORIGINAL TITLE	PORNification
Gremlins ⟶	*Rimlins*
Eight Legged Freaks ⟶	*Eight Leggy Freaks, Three Legged Freaks*
Children of the Corn ⟶	*Children of the Cornhole* (banned)

ORIGINAL TITLE		PORNification
Scream	⟶	*Cream*
Saw	⟶	*Spew*
Jaws	⟶	*Gums*

T_{ests}&A_{nswers}: Pornspotting

Which of these are actual produced porno's?
Answers found below.

Edward Penishands
Invasion of the Booty Snatchers
Total Reball
Scrotal Recall
Night of the Giving Head
Inrearendence Day

Answer:

They are all real except Scrotal Recall.

137

T$_{ests}$&A$_{nswers}$: Fun with Words

What word turns all of these into pornifications?
Answers on the following page.

The _____ *Guard*

American _____ (movie poster - A rose over a well-formed butt)

_____ *Double*

_____ *Shop*

Answer:

Booty

ORIGINAL TITLE	PORNification
The Neverending Story	*The Neverending Orgy,* *The Happyending Story*
I, Robot	*I, Ho-bot,* *I Rub It*
π	*Hair π*

ORIGINAL TITLE	PORNification
Harry Potter and the Sorcerer's Stone →	*Hairy Twatter and the Sorcerer's Bone*
Harry Potter and the Chamber of Secrets →	*Hairy Twatter and the Chamber of Secretions*
Harry Potter and the Prisoner of Azkaban →	*Hairy Twatter and the Prisoner of Asskebang*

ORIGINAL TITLE	PORNification
C.H.U.D. ⟶	*C.H.U.B.*
The Blob ⟶	*The Gob*
Brazil ⟶	*Brazilian, Bra? Nil*

Auto-Porn

(because some films come "pre-pornified")

The Black Hole

Contact

What Lies Beneath

Earth Girls are Easy

V

ORIGINAL TITLE	PORNification
Batman Begins ⟶	*Batman Finishes*
Sphere ⟶	*Cylinder*
Starship Troopers ⟶	*Starfish Poopers, Starfish Shtoopers*

Tests & Answers: Live Long and Prosper

Can you pornify the *Star Trek* Movies?

The Search for Spock

The Voyage Home

The Final Frontier

The Next Generation

Inner Sanctum

Answers:

The Search for Cock – The Voyeur's Home - The Anal Frontier - The Next Penetration - In-her-rectum

ORIGINAL TITLE		PORNification
Little Shop of Horrors	→	*Little Swap of Whores* (starring Rick More-anus)
House of Wax	→	*House of Whacks*
Creepshow	→	*Peepshow, Seepshow*

ORIGINAL TITLE **PORNification**

Freddy Vs. Jason ⟶ *Freddy Does Jason*

Alien Vs. Predator ⟶ *Alien Does Predator*

Hellraiser ⟶ *Swellraiser*

SCI-FI/HORROR

ORIGINAL TITLE	PORNification
12 Monkeys ⟶	*Spanking 12 Monkeys*
The Fifth Element ⟶	*The Filth Element*
Total Recall ⟶	*Throatal Recall*

T&A

Tests & Answers: Movie Plots

Here are the plots of three pornified movies. Can you give pornified titles for the plots described below?
Answers on the following page.

An organization with a secret agenda creates a super cyborg penis designed to tirelessly satisfy all women.

A short, wrinkled creature with a glowing shlong makes an extremely long distance phone sex call.

These girls are so exhausted, they can barely get you off, but they're gonna fight that fatigue and do the best they can! Hint: Tim Spurtin' directs Johnny Deep.

149

Answers:

Robocock (writes itself)

ET: The Extra Testicle / Eat Me, The Sexy-Terrestrial

Sleepy Swallow (for fatigue fetishists)

ORIGINAL TITLE	PORNification
Blair Witch Project ⟶	*Bare Bitch Project*
The Chronicles of Riddick ⟶	*The Conicals of BigDick*
The Omen ⟶	*The O' Men, The Hymen*

100% Real

(Actual Produced Porns)

The Sperminator
A Clockwork Orgy
Battlestar Orgasmica
Muffy the Vampire Layer
Ejacula
Interview With a Vibrator
Juranal Park
Erectnophobia
Planet of the Gapes
Men in Back
Whorelock
Rodzilla
I Know Who You Did Last Summer

Porns of M. Night Shyamalan

ORIGINAL TITLE	PORNification
The Village ⟶	*The Spillage*
Unbreakable ⟶	*Unfuckable*
The Sixth Sense ⟶	*The Sixth Inch, The Sixth Wench*

Fetish: Plumpers

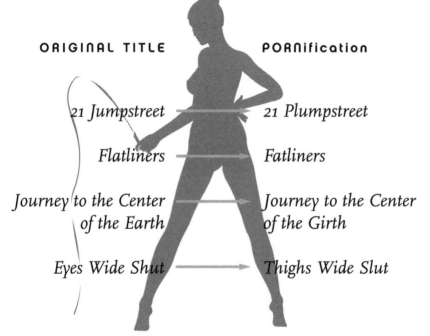

ORIGINAL TITLE

21 Jumpstreet

Flatliners

Journey to the Center of the Earth

Eyes Wide Shut

PORNification

21 Plumpstreet

Fatliners

Journey to the Center of the Girth

Thighs Wide Slut

chapter **8**

OPENING NIGHT:
MUSICALS & THEATER

ORIGINAL TITLE	PORNification
The Jazz Singer ⟶	*The Jizz Slinger*
Ragtime ⟶	*Gagtime*
Fiddler on the Roof ⟶	*Diddler on the Roof*

ORIGINAL TITLE	PORNification
Oklahoma! ⟶	*Oklahomo!*
Grease ⟶	*Crease,* *Lube*
Godspell ⟶	*Codsmell*

ORIGINAL TITLE	PORNification
Guys and Dolls →	*Guys and Balls, Guys and Inflatable Dolls*
Seven Brides for Seven Brothers →	*Seven Brides for Seven Brothas*
Bye Bye Birdie →	*Bi-Bi-Bernie*

T&A
Tests & Answers: Neil Semen

Pornify these Neil Semen plays to satisfy a boob fetish.
Answers found below.

Lost in Yonkers

The Odd Couple

Barefoot in the Park

Answers:

Lost in Honkers - The DD Couple - Baretit in the Park

ORIGINAL TITLE	PORNification
Annie Get Your Gun ⟶	*Annie Get My Bung*
The Sound of Music ⟶	*The Pound of Pubic,* *The Mound of Pubic,* *The Sound of Mucus*
Singin' in the Rain ⟶	*Singin' in Her Drain*

ORIGINAL TITLE	PORNification
Moulin Rouge ⟶	*Moulin Splooge*
The 3 Musketeers ⟶	*The 3 Muffkateers*
La Cage Aux Folles ⟶	*La Vag & Phallus,* *La Vag Aux Balls*

ORIGINAL TITLE	PORNification
M. Butterfly	M. Butterface
Rent	Spent, Bent
Cats	Pussies

Tests & Answers: Match the song

Match the pornified song with its pornified musical.
De-pornified answers on the following page.

Songs:

To Swallow

76 Rusty Trombones

All That Jizz

Bangtime for Hitler

*Ease on Down
the Load*

Titles:

Chica Go!, Chicaho

Little Oral Trannie

The Jiz

The Pubic Man

The Pro Doers

Answers:

Tomorrow – Little Orphan Annie (Annie)

76 Trombones – The Music Man

All That Jazz – Chicago

Springtime for Hitler – The Producers

Ease on Down the Road – The Wiz

ORIGINAL TITLE		PORNification
Purple Rain	⟶	*Purple Vein*
Saturday Night Fever	⟶	*Saturday Night Beaver*
Mo Better Blues	⟶	*Manbatter Blues, Ho Better Blow*

ORIGINAL TITLE	PORNification
The Phantom of the Opera ⟶	*The Precum of the Opera*
Thoroughly Modern Millie ⟶	*Thoroughly Done Millie*
Torch Song Trilogy ⟶	*Torch Song Thrill-Orgy*

Tests **&A**nswers: **Fun with Words**

What word turns all of these into pornifications?
Answers below.

_____ *in America*

City of _____

_____ *in the Outfield*

Answer:

Anals

167

Fetish: Animals

ORIGINAL TITLE

PORNification

Kangaroo Jack → *Kangaroo Jack-off*

Lassie → *Assie*

See Spot Run → *G Spot Fun*

Pelican Brief → *Pelican Queef*
(What? There's a market for a movie about the vaginal flatulence of a large sea bird.)

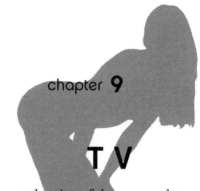

chapter **9**

TV

It's not the size of the screen that matters

ORIGINAL TITLE	PORNification
Will & Grace ⟶	*Fillin' Grace,* *Fillin' Face*
Yes, Dear ⟶	*Yes, Rear,* *Yes! Yes! Dear*
Punk'd ⟶	*Spunk'd*

ORIGINAL TITLE	PORNification
Saved by the Bell ⟶	*Shaved by the Balls*
Meet the Press ⟶	*Press the Meat*
Just Shoot Me ⟶	*Just Do Me,* *Just Shoot On Me*

TV

ORIGINAL TITLE	PORNification
Dynasty ⟶	*Da-Nasty*
The A-Team ⟶	*The A-Hole Team, The T&A Team*
The Three Stooges ⟶	*The Three Spooges*

T&A
Tests & Answers: Happy Lays

Can you pornify these *Happy Lays* spin-off's?
Answers found below.

Mork N' Mindy

Joanie Loves Chachi

Laverne and Shirley

Answers:

Porkin' Mindy - Joanie Loves Bukkake - Laverne Does Shirley

T V

173

ORIGINAL TITLE	PORNification
Win Ben Stein's Money →	*Win Ben Stein's Money Shot, Rim Ben Stein's Honey*
How I Met Your Mother →	*How I Did Your Mother*
Friends →	*Friends (with Benefits)*

ORIGINAL TITLE	PORNification
Lost ⟶	*Tossed, Lust*
Designing Women ⟶	*Reclining Women*
Desperate Housewives ⟶	*Really Desperate Housewives*

TV

175

T^{ests} & A^{nswers}: Pornspotting

Which of these are actual produced pornos?
Answers below.

> *Murphy Brown – Murphy's Brown*
> *NYPD Blue – NYDP Blue*
> *Knots Landing – Knots Landing Strip*
> *Seinfeld – Mindfelch*
> *The Nanny – The Fanny*
> *The Flintstones – The Flintbones*
> *The Honeymooners – The Horny-Mooners*
> *Quantam Leap – Quantum Deep*
> *Three Wishes – Three Squishes*
> *Everybody Loves Raymond – Everybody Loves Rimmin'*

Answers:

Knots Landing Strip, Mindfelch, and *Three Squishes* are not real. The rest are actual produced films.

176

ORIGINAL TITLE	PORNification
The Love Boat ⟶	*The Love Throat*
Matlock ⟶	*Fatcock*
My Three Sons ⟶	*My Three-somes*

TV

ORIGINAL TITLE	PORNification
Howdy Doody →	*How'd He Do Me?*
I Love Lucy →	*I Love Juicy,* *I Love Loosely,* *I Love Poosy*
America's Next *Top Model* →	*America's Next* *Bottom Model*

Auto-Porn

(because some films come pre-pornified)

Bosom Buddies

Head of the Class

Eight Is Enough

The Unit

ORIGINAL TITLE	PORNification
Full House ⟶	*Full Blouse,* *Full Mouth*
The Golden Girls ⟶	*The Golden Shower Girls*
What's Happenin'!!! ⟶	*What's Splatterin'!!!*

ORIGINAL TITLE	PORNification
Bewitched ⟶	*Sandwiched*
Entertainment Tonight ⟶	*EnterTenMen Tonight*
The Sopranos ⟶	*The Sopornos*

TV

ORIGINAL TITLE	PORNification
Spin City ⟶	*Sit and Spin City*
H.R. Pufnstuf ⟶	*H.R. MuffnStuff*
The Fresh Prince ⟶	*The Fresh Prince Albert of Bel Air*

The Most Pornified TV Show Ever

According to "research", *I Dream Of Genie* is the most pornified show ever, with at least 11 actually produced pornifications.

I Cream Of Genie
I Cream Of Jeannie
I Cream On Genie
I Cream On Jeannie
I Cream With Genie
I Scream For Genie
Bi Dream Of Genie
I Ream A Genie
I Dream Of Jenna
I Dream Of Queenie
I Dream of Weenie

ORIGINAL TITLE	PORNification
SpongeBob Squarepants →	*Bung-throb, Pear Pants*
M*A*S*H →	*G*A*S*H*
American Idol →	*ATMerican Idol*

ORIGINAL TITLE	PORNification
NUMB3RS ⟶	*THUMB3RS*
Simon & Simon ⟶	*Semen & Semen, Hymen & Hymen*
Cagney and Lacey ⟶	*Gag-me and Lay-me* (s&m fetish)

TV

Car Make Pornifications

Ford Clitaurus

Geo Jism

Chevy Astro Glide

Dodge Butt Dart

Ford Poontang

Chrysler Le Bare Ass

Ford Escort Service

Ford Sexplorer

Toyota Gland Cruiser

Volkswagen Grab-it

Lincoln Town Whore

Oldsmobile Butt Lass

Honda Prelube

Flex Your Muscle

These stumped us. See what you can come up with...

Life Is Beautiful
Peggy Sue Got Married
Pleasantville
Pocketful of Miracles
Viva Las Vegas
Monsoon Wedding
The Crying Game
The Apostle
Like Water For Chocolate
Out Of Sight
Prizzi's Honor
Shampoo

TV

ORIGINAL TITLE	PORNification
Mad About You ⟶	*Nad About You,* *Mad About Spew*
Dragnet ⟶	*Drag Net*
Cheers ⟶	*Queers,* *Cheeks*

Tests & Answers: As Kinky as You Want to Be

Pornify the following movies to find a bizarre fetish!
Answers on the following page.

Mean Girls
There's Something About Mary
Rush Hour
Dreamweaver
The Man Who Wasn't There
Far From Heaven
Quigley Down Under
Hercules
Jungle Fever
The Shaggy Dog
Gleaming The Cube

TV

T&A
Tests & Answers: As Kinky as You Want to Be

Answer:
They are all for pubic hair fetishists.

Mean Curls
There's Something about Hairy
Bush Hour, Bush Shower
Dreambeaver
The Man Who Wasn't Bare
Far from Shaven
Squiggly Down Under
Her Curlies
Jungle Beaver
The Shaggy Log
Gleaming The Pubes

Books

If you're reading this book, you probably haven't read many others. Perhaps if they had been pornified, you would have been more interested.

Fiction:

For Whom The Belle Blows

A Connecticut Yankee in King Arthur's Throat

Uncle Tom's Cabana

Jane Eyriola

Pair-a-guys Tossed

Madam Ovaries

Da Kinki Coed

To Catch Her in the Eye

Dart of Darkness

Non-fiction:

Who's You Rich Daddy, Who's Your Poor Daddy?

The Seven Habits of Highly Erective People

Who Fucked My Cheese?

TV

T&A ests nswers: Something in Common

Can you pornify the following works and name their author? Answers found below.

Oliver Twist
A Tale of Two Cities
David Copperfield
Great Expectations
Hard times
Nicholas Nickleby

Answer:

Charles Dick-ins (Dickens)

All-of-her Fist - *A Tale of Two Titties* - *David Cop-a-feel* - *Great Sexpectations* - *Hard Times* (autoporn) - *Knickerless Nickelby* (that's one you can tell your mom, nice and clean)

Fetish: Mature

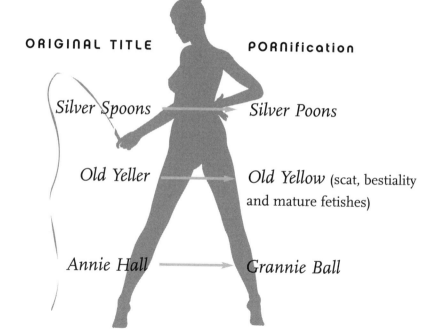

ORIGINAL TITLE

Silver Spoons

Old Yeller

Annie Hall

PORNification

Silver Poons

Old Yellow (scat, bestiality and mature fetishes)

Grannie Ball

chapter **10**

ƒLOPPY ƒECONDƒ

Miscellaneous Pornifications and Quizzes

ORIGINAL TITLE	PORNification
House Of Flying Daggers ⟶	*Mouth of Flying Daggers*
The Endless Summer ⟶	*The Endless Hummer*
A Star is Born ⟶	*A Star Is Torn*

T&A
ests nswers: Sex Degrees of Kevin Bacon

Can you connect Kevin Bacon with Hairyass Ford?
Answer below.

Hairyass Ford starred in *Star Whores* with James Earl Bones...

Who starred in *Gonad the Barbarian* with Arnold Schwartzenpecker...

Who starred in *Twins* (autoporn) with Danny DPto...

Who starred in *One Spewed Over the Cookoo's Breast* with Jack Nippleson...

Who starred in *A Few Goo'd Men* with...

Kevin Bacon!

ORIGINAL TITLE	PORNification
Get Shorty ⟶	*Get My Shorty* (starring John Travulva)
Run Lola Run ⟶	*Cum Lola Cum,* *Run Lolita Run*
The League of *Extraordinary* *Gentlemen* ⟶	*The League of* *Extraordinary* *Genitalmen*

ORIGINAL TITLE		PORNification
Last Tango in Paris	⟶	*Ass Tango In Paris*
Desperately Seeking Susan	⟶	*Desperately Seeking Semen*
The Love Bug	⟶	*The Love Tug*

T^{ests}&A_{nswers}: Two Can Make a Difference

Each of the following titles can be pornified by adding one of the sets of two letters to it.   The letters may be added to the beginning, middle or end of the title.
Answers found below.

Doctor Who   *(te)*

The Greatest American Hero   *(sp)*

Ray   *(re)*

Answers:

Doctor Who(re) - The Greatest American He(te)ro - (Sp)ray

100% REAL (Actual Produced Porns)

Cheeks And Thong Up In Stroke

Dial E For Enema

Dial A For Anal

The Mighty Phucks

Dude, Where's My Dildo?

Hillstreet Blacks

Tits A Wonderful Life

Leave It To Cleavage

2069: A Sex Odyssey

Sweet Ho Alabama

T&A nswers: High Concept Porn

Give the pornified title to the plots described below.
Answers on the following page.

A man has to convince a woman over and over to have sex with him, as she loses her memory at orgasm.

Upon orgasm, a woman finds herself having sex again with the same man, and has to relive it in all sorts of different ways over and over.

A man gets a remote control that allows him to control his sex life, pausing, rewinding, using slow-motion, etc.

A woman find her self post-coitus. We trace backwards to discover the events that led up to the climax.

T&A: High Concept Porn

Tests & Answers

Answers:

50 First Dates ⟶ *50 Forced Dates*

Groundhog Day ⟶ *Poundflog Day*

Click ⟶ *Prick*

Memento ⟶ *Semento*

T&A
Tests & Answers: What's in a Name?

Pick the bona fide porn stars. Answers found below.

Arnold Schwartzenpecker

Britney Rears

REDDD FOXXX

Fudge Reinhold

Jerk Douglas

Prince Albert Brooks

Gene Hardman

Pee Wee Spermin'

AtoM Arkin

Angelina Jolly

Answer:

Arnold Schwartzenpecker, Britney Rears, Jerk Douglas, Gene Hardman, Angelina Jolly are all real. The others are fake.

ORIGINAL TITLE	PORNification
Monster-In-Law →	*Monster-In-Jaw*
One Hour Photo →	*One Hour Porno*
Millers Crossing →	*Spillers Crossing*

Richard Gear Vehicles:

Desperate Mouselives

Rodent to Perdition

Of Mice in Men

Full Mouse

Passion of the Mice

Stuart Little 3

Sports

Eight Men Out	→	*Eight Men In*
He Got Game	→	*He Got Gay*
The Karate Kid	→	*The Bukkake Kid*
Major League	→	*Major Leg;* *Major League Ass,* *Labia Majoris League*
Searching For Bobby Fischer	→	*Searching For Bobbi's Fissure*
The Natural	→	*The Naturals*
Rookie of the Year	→	*Nookie of the Year*
Hoosiers	→	*Ho-siers,* *Hoosier Daddy's*
Raging Bull	→	*Raging Balls*

De-pornification

Mainstream cinema is not always averse to innuendo. Witness the de-pornifications of these Bond women.

Pussy Galore ⟶ *Patsy Gilford*

Honey Ryder ⟶ *Bonnie Rifkin*

Holly Goodhead ⟶ *Hillary Goodwyn*

ORIGINAL TITLE	PORNification
The Good, the Bad, and the Ugly ⟶	*The Good, the Bad, and the Orgy*
Westworld ⟶	*Breastworld*
Once Upon a Time in the West ⟶	*Once Upon a Time In the* (insert any orifice)

Rare Native American Porno

ORIGINAL TITLE	PORNification
Dances with Wolves ⟶	*Lapdances with Wolves*
Black Hawk Down ⟶	*Black Hawk Goes Down, Black Cock Down*
The Last of the Mohicans ⟶	*The Lust of the Hohicans, The Lust of the Mo'cheekin's, The Lust of Mo Cheeks*

Video Game Pornifications

Fudgepack-man

Wang Commander

Beaverquest

Grand Theft Autoeroticasphyxiation

Mike Tyson's Donkey Punch-Out

Missile Demand

Dong

RimCity

Pubic The Wedgehog

Face Invaders

Whorecraft

Dribblization

Badonkadonk-ey Kong

ORIGINAL TITLE	PORNification
Up The Creek ⟶	*Up the Crack*
Revenge of the Nerds ⟶	*Revenge of the Nads*
Dirty Dancing ⟶	*Dirty Sanchezing*

World Worst Pornifications

Hemorrhoids of a Geisha

Finding Nimoy

Lumpy Old Men

A.I. – Artificial Insemination

Lake Flaccid

Sines

Cystic Shiver

SpongeBoob Squaretits

Ordinary Pee-hole

Suturama

The Sixth Mensch

T_{ests} &A_{nswers}: Fun with Words

What unit of measurement can replace those in the titles below to create instant pornifications?

Answers on the following page.

Six _____ Under

8 _____

The Whole Nine _____

Tests & Answers: Fun with Words

Answer:

Inches

ORIGINAL TITLE		PORNification
The Butterfly Effect	→	*The Butterface Effect*
K-Pax	→	*KY Packs*
Phonebooth	→	*Pornbooth*

ORIGINAL TITLE	PORNification
Hudsucker Proxy ⟶	*Pud-sucker Foxy*
Napoleon Dynamite ⟶	*Napoleon Sodomite*
Catch Me If You Can ⟶	*Felch Me If You Can*

ORIGINAL TITLE	PORNification
Gunga Din →	*Gunga-ed In*
Indecent Proposal →	*Indecent Disposal*
The Cisco Kid →	*The Crisco Kid*

ABOUT THE AUTHOR
Andrew Benjamin

I know what you are thinking: this dude has way too much time on his hands. Actually, nothing could be further from the truth. When not wallowing in the gutter, Andrew Benjamin is the COO of an internet company (who threatened to fire him if named), lives in a co-op in NYC (whose board promised to evict him if named) and serves on the board of his house of worship (whose leadership made it abundantly clear they would excommunicate him if named). Andrew is married to a wonderful woman (who swore to divorce him if named), has supportive parents (who will disinherit him if named), and is currently expecting his first child (who is as yet, unnamed).

Email me. After all, what's the worst than can happen?: AB@pornifythis.com

Submit your own pornification at www.pornifythis.com

Got your own pornification?

Submit it at:
www.pornifythis.com.

ACKNOWLEDGMENTS

I would like to acknowledge all the people who contributed to this book... but for some reason they have all requested to remain anonymous. So my thanks go out to:

Slim Jim, The Lone B & Donnajew, Big Daddy Magni, Ben Wa, and last but certainly not least, Street Papa the master spornifier for his unique ability to pornify sports themed movies.

The editors of this book would like to acknowledge Tony Salah and Dan Binstock for their many contributions.

Other Books by Falls Media:

**From the authors of the hit *Would You Rather...?*® book series
comes a whole new collection of deranged dilemmas.**

Would You Rather...?: Love & Sex asks you to ponder such questions as:

- **Would you rather...** orgasm once every ten years OR
  once every ten seconds?

- **Would you rather...** have to have sex in the same
  position every night OR have to have sex in a different
  position every night (you can never repeat)?

- **Would you rather...** have breast implants made of Nerf® OR
  Play - Doh®?

- **Would you rather...** have sex with the new Daisy Duke (Jessica Simpson) OR
  Classic Daisy Duke (Catherine Bach)?

- **Would you rather...** vicariously experience all orgasms that occur in your zip code OR
  during sex, have the Microsoft paper clip help icon appear with sex tips?

Would You Rather...?: Love & Sex can be read alone or played together as a game.   Laugh-out-loud
funny, uniquely imaginative, and deceptively thought-provoking, ***Would You Rather: Love & Sex*** is
simultaneously the authors most mature and immature work yet!

Available at www.wouldyourather.com

Would You Rather...?® 2: Electric Boogaloo

Another collection of over three hundred absurd alternatives and demented dilemmas. Filled with wacky wit, irreverent humor and twisted pop-culture references.

The Official Movie Plot Generator

"A Coffee Table Masterpiece" - *Newsweek*.

The Official Movie Plot Generator is a unique and interactive humor book that offers 27,000 hilarious movie plot possibilities you create, spanning every genre of cinema from feel-good family fun to hard-boiled crime drama to soft-core pornography. Just flip the book's ninety tabs until you find a plot combination you like. For movie fans or anyone who likes to laugh a lot with little effort, *The Official Movie Plot Generator* is a perfect gift and an irresistible, offbeat diversion.

Available at www.wouldyourather.com